ARIO MERZ : WHAT IS TO BE DONE ?

The Henry Moore Institute is a world-recognised centre for the study of sculpture. An award-winning exhibitions venue, research centre, library and sculpture archive, the Institute hosts a year-round programme of exhibitions, conferences and lectures, as well as developing research and publications, to expand the understanding and scholarship of historical and contemporary sculpture.

The Henry Moore Foundation was founded by the sculptor Henry Moore (1898–1986) in 1977 to encourage the appreciation of the visual arts, especially sculpture. The Institute is a part of the Foundation, and is tasked with the responsibility to study sculpture. Its role is to make a significant impact on the future of art history through a programme that consistently re-thinks how we understand sculpture today. The starting point for all of our activities is the artwork. To study sculpture is to consider how the artwork operates in space; to understand sculpture, direct encounter is essential.

The *Essays on Sculpture* series is published three times a year, presenting scholarly texts relating to our exhibitions, research and to the Leeds Museums and Galleries sculpture collections, which are managed in partnership with the Institute, a partnership which has built one of the strongest public collections of sculpture in Britain. Written by Institute staff, visiting scholars, artists, guest curators and invited writers, *Essays on Sculpture* focus on the ways in which sculpture – be it historical, modern or contemporary – reverberates in the present.

The *Essays* take unexpected routes through definitions of sculpture. In No. 15, for example, Joy Sleeman takes as her point of departure a pot made by Richard Long that was acquired for the Leeds collections in 1996 as a means to consider Long's early work. In No. 39, Matthew Withey looks at sculpture and socialism in Britain in the mid-twentieth century. In No. 55, Jon Wood addresses the literal drawing on sculpture as artists and others intervene on surfaces – invited and otherwise. As with all of the Institute's activities, the *Essays* seek to raise more questions than answers, and to complicate the ways in which sculpture is understood and defined. This sixty-third issue is published on the occasion of our exhibition *Mario Merz: What Is to Be Done?* This essay and exhibition focus on Merz's sculptures made between 1966 and 1977, paying attention to the ways in which the Italian artist used materials as 'protagonists'.

The *Essays on Sculpture* are available from the Institute Bookshop and through our website. The series can be subscribed to in issues of five, at a cost of £20, and all subscribers are sent two back issues of their choice free of charge. Back issues are available for purchase (see p. 29) with all issues, including those out of print, collected in the Institute's Research Library. Our sixty-fourth issue will be published in Autumn 2011.

Lisa Le Feuvre
HEAD OF SCULPTURE STUDIES
HENRY MOORE INSTITUTE

Protagonist materials

Mario Merz (1925–2003) rethought the possibilities of sculpture, working from observation to propose an invigorated way of perceiving the surrounding world, stripped of convention and firmly embedded in the present. Drawing together incompatible materials into groups of meaning, his constructions are sculptural proposals for considering how objects are used to negotiate our place in the world. Merz used materials as 'protagonists', active agents driving sculptural attitudes and forms through process and proliferation. This *Essay on Sculpture* accompanies an exhibition at the Henry Moore Institute focusing on the artist's sculptural production between 1966 and 1977. Recurring forms and concerns characterise Merz's artistic practice – his use of neon, beginning in 1966; the igloo, starting in 1968; numerical progressions, used from 1970; and the question 'what is to be done?', employed from 1967. This latter preoccupation is taken as the title of this exhibition.

'What is to be done?' – or '*Che fare?*' – is a question central to Merz's approach to art making. Based in Turin, he was a key figure in *Arte Povera*, a term coined by the critic Germano Celant to describe a loose grouping of artists working in 1960s Italy. This was a time of social, political and artistic upheaval as Italy dealt with the consequences of the post-war 'economic miracle' of the 1950s that polarised economic inequalities. Merz was driven by asking what an artist can do in the face of a precarious future, informed by an examination of the role of art in day-to-day human experience and motivated by the belief that an artist can show something otherwise impossible to explain.[1] For Merz, to be an artist was to offer questions rather than answers. To work without an assumption of structure, conduct, prediction or outcome, the artist must stretch beyond the limits of the present: in any version of the present, the future is uncertain, conditioned by speculation and interpretations of the past. Two works bear the question 'what is to be done?' in this exhibition. In '*Che fare?*' (1968–73) [Cat. 6] the title is written in neon, sitting atop a bed of wax held in an aluminium cooking pot. As the neon warms the wax, it appears to melt and emit a smell. '*Che fare?*' (after 1967) [Cat. 4] asks the question again in blue neon, this time hung on the wall. Here at

1 'Mario Merz at the Whitechapel Gallery' in *Audio Arts*, vol. 5, no. 2, 1980.

6

Mario Merz (1925–2003)

Che fare?

(What is to be done? 1968–73)

4

Mario Merz

Che fare?

(What is to be done? After 1967)

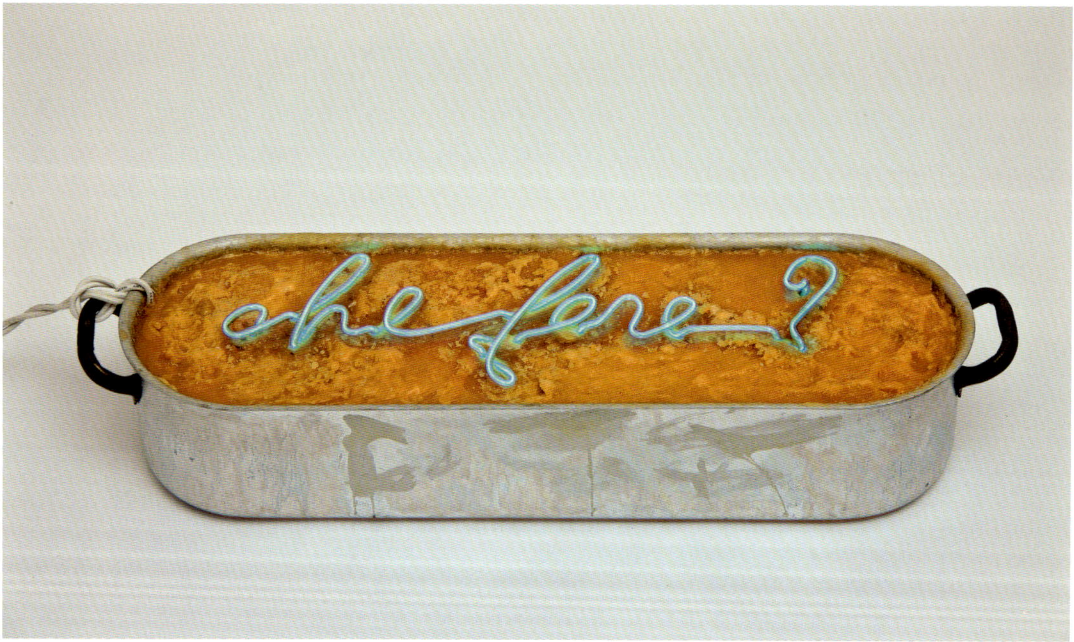

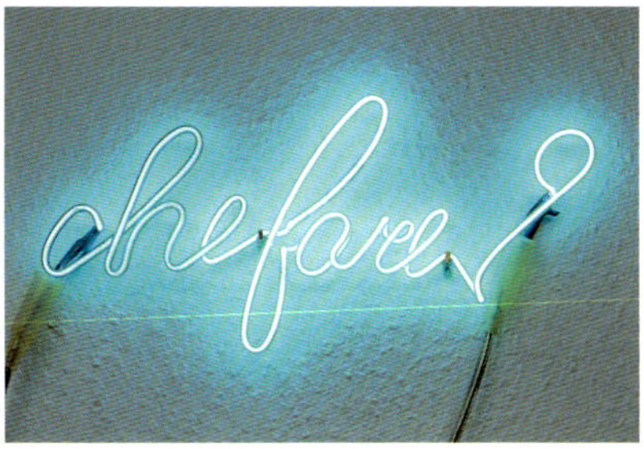

the Institute, it confronts the visitor immediately on entering the gallery spaces. In both works the text is modelled on Merz's own writing in a continuous flow, as if the hand forming it had not lifted from the page.

The statement 'what is to be done?' is one much referenced, and much misused, in art and its surrounding discourses. It is most associated with a 1902 political pamphlet by Vladimir Lenin, the title appropriated from an 1863 socialist novel by Nikolay Chernyshevsky written from a position where art was believed 'a medium for revealing, vicariously experiencing, and thereby better understanding reality. Reality itself could not be transcended, only comprehended.'[2] These attitudes reverberate through Merz's work. Lenin's text was translated from Russian into Italian relatively late in 1968 by Luciano Gruppi. Merz, however, claimed that he had little interest in it – confiding in an interview in 2003 that he only ever read Lenin's pamphlet in a bookshop and that he had developed an interest in the question by observing children at play constantly asking 'what is to be done?'[3] Artists, though, are not always to be trusted and it is most likely that he will have read the text when first translated.

Merz's early years were charged by their political surroundings. He was born in Milan and grew up in Turin during Mussolini's harshest years, where his Swiss father designed engines for the Fiat factory and his mother taught music. He began his career as a medical student, leaving Università degli Studi di Torino after two years to be an activist in the socialist group *Giustizia e Libertà* (Justice and Liberty); in 1945 he was arrested and imprisoned for a year for party leafleting. In a number of interviews Merz described how while in prison he began to draw, frequently noting his first drawing was of a bearded fellow-prisoner made by never lifting the pencil from the page – a strategy that would return later in the continuous light-writing. In repeatedly returning to this anecdote, Merz carefully framed his own work as a practice rooted in an activist past. On release he continued to draw, these early drawings of grasses made by never lifting his hand from the page. These were first published in 1969 in *l'Unita*, the Italian Communist Party's newspaper. This methodology

2 Katz, Michael R., and William G. Wagner, 'Chernyshevsky, *What Is to Be Done?* and the Russian Intelligentsia', Introduction to Chernyshevsky, Nikolai, *What Is to Be Done?* Cornell University Press, New York, 1989, p. 17.

3 Eccher, Danilo, 'A Conversation with Mario Merz' in *Mario Merz*, exh. cat., Fundación Proa, Buenos Aires, 2003, p. 25.

he describes as a means to record both what he could see, and the time and experience of depiction. Continuous practice resonating with context is at the core of Merz's work. For him, artwork should at all times be grounded in human experience.

In 1950 he began painting, with his first solo exhibition in 1954 at Galleria La Bussola in Turin. Our exhibition begins in 1966 when Merz turned his attention to sculpture, moving away from earlier expressionist experiments, joining the forward-looking Galleria Gian Enzo Sperone in Turin.[4] Utilising natural, domestic and industrial materials that were ready at hand, Merz removed their functionality through unfamiliar juxtapositions, with the neon shooting energy into inert materials – 'a kind of thunderbolt that would enter objects'.[5] '*Salamino*' ('Small Salami', 1966) [Cat. 1], for example, is formed from a rolled and tied blanket cut with a spear of neon angled from the left, with cables stretching out to power sources above and below. The blanket was made by the artist Marisa Merz (b. 1931), Merz's wife who had a keen influence on the development of his work. The work recalls both the bundles carried by nomads, and the Italian domestic image of a sausage hanging to dry in a pantry. '*Bottiglia*' ('Bottle', 1967) [Cat. 2] likewise transforms and energises the commonplace through the injection of light: a green wine bottle attached to a shelf, pointing neck downwards, is pierced with white neon curving its way into the bottle, the neon inside glowing green from the glass. Light rather than wine spills into perception: as Merz notes 'wine represents energy that passes through the body and alters feelings and perceptions'.[6] Such a seemingly throwaway comment reaches to Merz's sculptural concerns: for him, the direct encounter has the ability to undo assumptions of perception.

Merz's sculptures are objects set into motion by being perceived, unfolding in relation to surrounding architecture and attitudes, testing and extending possibilities of form. Neon operates using low energy pulses, and requires power cables stretching to sockets and heavy, now obsolete, electrical transformers. In these works there is no artifice – it is obvious

4 Opening in the same building as the Italian Communist Party in 1963, the gallery was committed to showing artists who stretched definitions of artistic practice. Merz's first solo exhibition of his sculptural work took place there in 1968. See Minola, Anna, *Gian Enzo Sperone-Turin-Rome-New York: 35 Years of Exhibitions Between Europe and America*, Hopefulmonster, Turin, 2000.

5 Celant, Germano, 'Interview with Mario Merz, Genoa 1971' in *Mario Merz*, exh. cat., The Solomon R. Guggenheim Foundation, New York/Electa, Milan, 1988. pp. 104–5.

6 Ibid.

1

Mario Merz

Salamino

(Small Salami, 1966)

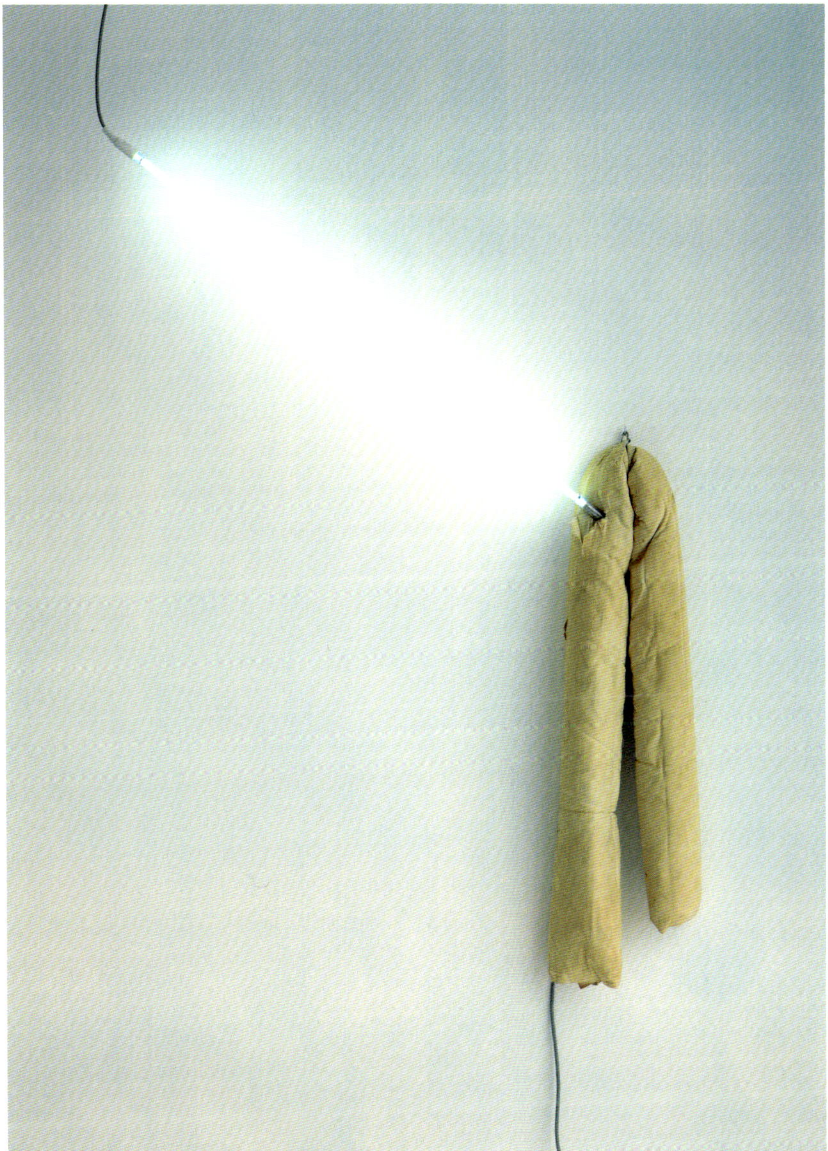

2

Mario Merz

Bottiglia

(Bottle, 1967)

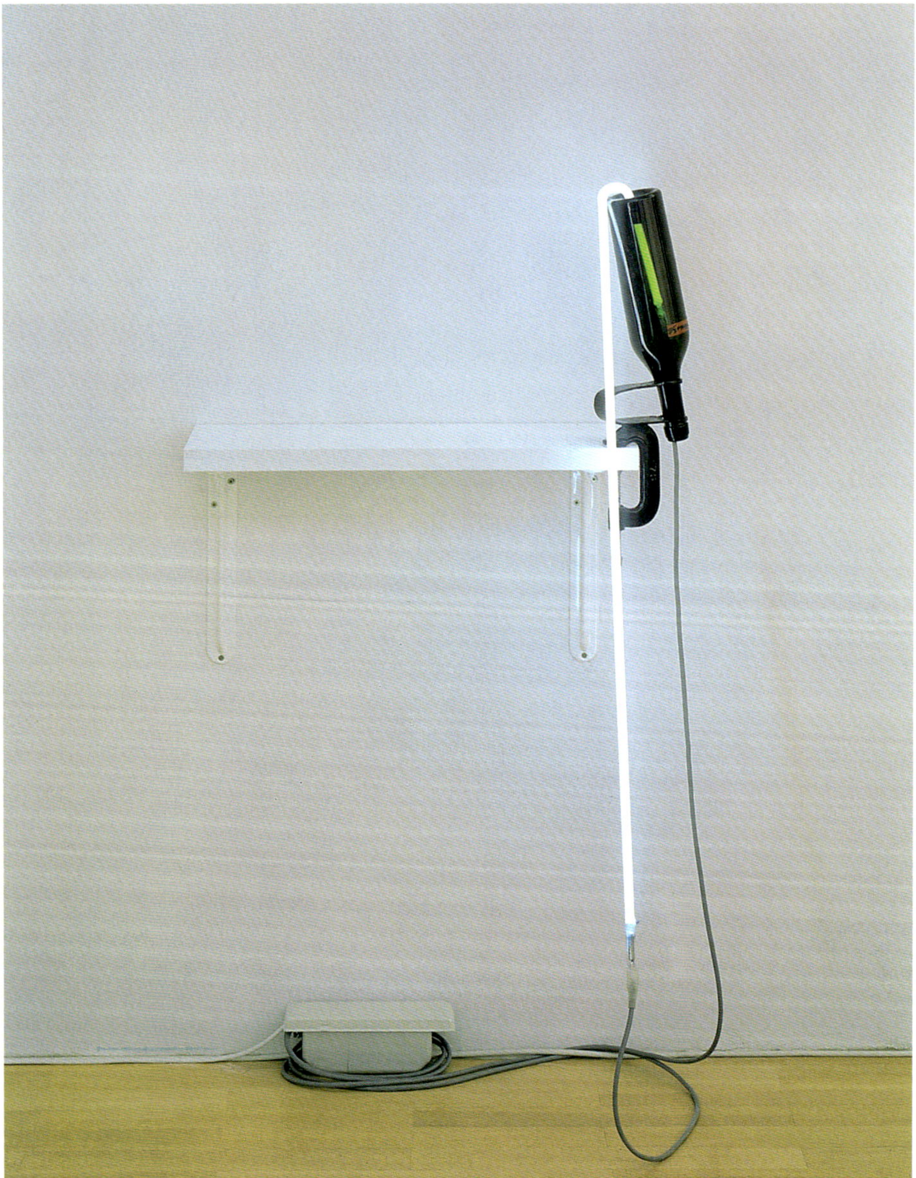

that if one turns off the power the lights would turn to dark. Germano Celant describes visiting the studio of Marisa and Mario Merz in 1966 to find 'straw-and-neon structures (now lost) and aluminium snails'.[7] He also recalls visiting Merz's first solo exhibition at Galleria Sperone in 1968 where he was struck by Merz's use of neon tubes, 'not the mass produced version used by Dan Flavin, but the free-form type used in advertising',[8] that made the exhibition 'a fireworks of pieces: the fluorescent tubes passed through bottles, glasses and cones as if they were an eruption of wine and lava [...] The luminosity caused everything to boil visually.'[9]

1966 is the year Celant describes as 'the debut of *Arte Povera*'.[10] In the year between these two encounters with Merz's work, September 1967, Celant curated the exhibition *Arte Povera e IM spazio*[11] at Galleria La Bertesca in Genoa. The accompanying catalogue, consisting of seven sheets in a folder, had two sections – *Arte Povera*[12] and *IM spazio*. The former included his first text titled '*Arte Povera*' where he announced: 'the commonplace has entered the sphere of art. The insignificant has begun to exist – indeed it has imposed itself.'[13] Although his work was clearly known by Celant, Merz was not included in this exhibition, but was cited in the polemical essay-manifesto[14] *Arte Povera: Notes for a Guerrilla War* published in the November-December issue of the Italian magazine *Flash Art*. Celant's use of this term *arte povera* in these two texts formulated what is now regarded as an art historical movement in art. *Arte Povera* literally translates as 'poor art', but crucially *povera* refers to objects activated through use, rather than to a paucity of wealth. *Povera* materials are 'protagonists'. In *Arte Povera: Notes for a Guerrilla War* Celant describes, in forceful language,[15] Merz's use of light as actively engaging with physical and social processes, claiming the perceptual field by 'violat[ing] objects and reality with neon. He pins his objects down dramatically, striking them with terror.'[16] Celant's term was inspired by the theatre director Jerzy Grotowski's (1933–2009) notion of 'Poor Theatre' that made a distinction from the spectacle of television and film. Staging was stripped back to communicate complex ideas using an economy of means to confront assumptions and address imponderables. Grotowski noted:

7 Celant, Germano, 'How to escape from the hallucinations of history' in *Arte Povera. Histories and Protagonists*, Electa, Milan, 1985, p. 22.

8 'Sphere of Influence: Germano Celant on Mario Merz', *Artforum*, January 2004, p. 25.

9 Ibid., p. 25–6.

10 Celant, Germano, 'The Organic Flow of Art' in *Mario Merz*, exh. cat., The Solomon R. Guggenheim Foundation, New York/Electa, Milan, 1988, p. 21.

11 *IM spazio* is a shortened form of *immagine spazio* – 'image space'.

12 With contributions by Alighiero Boetti, Luciano Fabro, Jannis Kounellis, Giulio Paolini, Pino Pascali and Emilio Prini.

13 Celant, Germano, '*Arte Povera IM Spazio*' reprinted in '1967–1971' in *Arte Povera. Histories and Protagonists*, Electa, Milan, 1985, p. 31.

14 As described by Celant: Celant, Germano, 'How to escape from the hallucinations of history' in *Arte Povera. Histories and Protagonists*,

7
Mario Merz
Automobile trapassata dal neon
(Automobile pierced by neon, 1969/1982)

Electa, Milan, 1985, p. 22.
15 See Cullinan, Nicholas, 'From Vietnam to Fiat-nam: The Politics of Arte Povera' in *October*, Spring 2008, no. 124.
16 Celant, Germano, 'Arte Povera: Notes for a Guerrilla War' in *Flash Art* n.5, 1967, reprinted in '1967–1971' in *Arte Povera. Histories and Protagonists*, Electa, Milan, 1985, p. 37.
17 See Grotowski, Jerzy, 'Towards a Poor Theatre' in *Towards a Poor Theatre*, Odin Teatrets Forlag, Holstebro, 1968, reprinted Methuen Drama, London, 1991, p. 24.
18 Ibid., p. 19.
19 See Arendt, Hannah, 'The Crisis in Culture: Its Social and Its Political Significance', in *Between Past and Future: Six Exercises in Political Thought*, Penguin Books, 1993, pp. 197–226.
20 Thompson, Jon, 'New times, new thoughts, new Sculpture' in *Gravity and Grace: the Changing Condition of Sculpture 1965–75*, exh. cat., Hayward Gallery, London, 1993, p. 14.
21 'Questions to Stella and

> We are bound, unconsciously or consciously, to be influenced by the traditions, in science and in art, even by the suspicions and presentiments peculiar to the civilization that has moulded us, just as we breathe the air of the particular continent that has given us life.[17]

He considered theatre a laboratory for thought defined by 'perceptual, direct, "live" communication'[18] initiated by the encounter between actor and spectator. For Grotowski the work – in his case theatre, in ours sculpture – must be experienced directly to be engaged with. Corporeal experience in space makes sculpture do its 'work'. Celant called for attention to be paid to an emerging force of *arte povera* within the field of visual art that stepped aside from the universalising principles of popular culture and industrialisation, placing art within the world and making a clear distinction between 'art' and 'culture'.[19]

Considering Merz's work today is to look at his work through the lens of *Arte Povera* where artists employed functional materials not valued for use in artworks and to the radical political changes that occurred in the late 1960s. As Jon Thompson notes, sculpture in this period was defined by the context of the transformations taking place socially, politically and artistically as artists wrestled with 'how to position oneself as an artist in relation to the pressing political realities governing society at large.'[20] In Europe, this was a moment of anti-American thought, in terms of both the Vietnam War and the domination of art world discourses by a North American voice. Donald Judd, for example, claimed in 1968 no interest in European art, saying 'It suits me fine if it all goes down the drain',[21] while amid city-wide protests students from the Committee of Students, Workers and Revolutionary Intellectuals called for a boycott of the 1968 *Venice Biennale*, criticising it as a 'tourist activity destined for the rich… enrich[ing] the great hotel companies together with the big industries which exploit labour'.[22] As a result twenty-three of the Italian artists participating the *Biennale* closed their rooms. Celant's text was a call for a simultaneous revolution in art and politics.

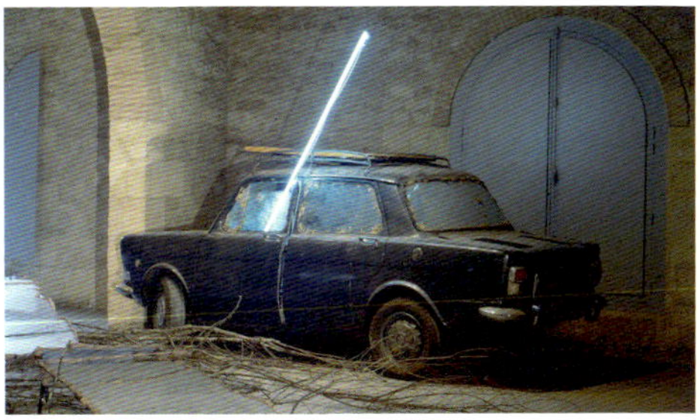

Merz's materials range across those seen in this exhibition – wicker, blankets, iron tubing, sheets of glass, stucco, wax, neon, wood shavings, bottles – to pillows, newspapers, social events set around tables and brushwood. Such materials are inert until released into the world: newspapers are carriers of information with a power far beyond paper and ink; brushwood is used to make fire; social events generate action. Merz gathered combative combinations that fed off their specific associations. His choices are based on form and on content – in other words, forms are selected for their productive ability. This is the distinction between material and *protagonist* material.

Merz released his objects into the world to complicate what is already known, intertwining the sculptural object with thought and perception. This can explicitly be seen in an exhibition titled *Che fare?* in 1969 at Galleria L'Attico in Rome, a former garage. Merz wrote *Che fare?* in mud on the gallery wall above an open tap, the water flowing out into a bucket and over the edges into the gutter. The question in this context was simple: here is a problem, what should be done to resolve it? This is the most basic definition of intellectual thought. In this situation *Che fare?* was directed to the water, and it was to observe rather than give a solution. Merz explored transformation of materials by use: in the three '*Che fare?*' works cited, heat, illumination and unchecked water are unleashed to produce a state of affairs where materials are employed for effect rather than form. Merz arrived to install this exhibition from Zurich in his Simca 1000 car. Nimble, rear-engined and budget, the French vehicle was equipped with four doors, roof rack and Swiss registration plates. Merz parked it in the gallery, front bumper just touching the wall and loaded the roof rack with six panes of glass stacked in a pair, on top of which sat an undulating sheet of wax. He then speared an arrow of neon through the driver's side window. This became '*Automobile trapassata dal neon*' ('Automobile pierced by neon', 1969/82) [Cat. 7].[23] Eleven works in total were shown in *Che fare?* including '*Torciglione*' ('Helicoil', 1969) [Cat. 8] that is also included here in *Mario Merz: What Is to Be Done?* This tall sculpture leans on the wall, made from

Judd', interview by Bruce Glaser, edited by Lucy R. Lippard in Battock, Gregory, (ed.), *Minimal Art: a critical anthology*, University of California Press, Berkeley, Los Angeles and London, 1968, p. 154, originally the discussion was broadcast on WBAI-FM, New York, February 1964, as 'New Nihilism or New Art?'.

22 From a pamphlet *Workmen Companions* cited in Alloway, Lawrence, *The Venice Biennale 1895–1968: from salon to goldfish bowl*, New York Graphic Society Ltd, Greenwich, Connecticut, 1968, p. 25.

23 In 1982 the work was remade by CAPC Musée d'art contemporain de Bordeaux, under the direction of the artist, for the exhibition *Antiform, Arte Povera: Sculptures 1966–1969*. Merz wrote by hand on the rear registration plate of the Simca '*au bord d'eau*' (the edge of the water) as a play on words with 'Bordeaux'.

3

Mario Merz

Cono

(Cone, c.1967)

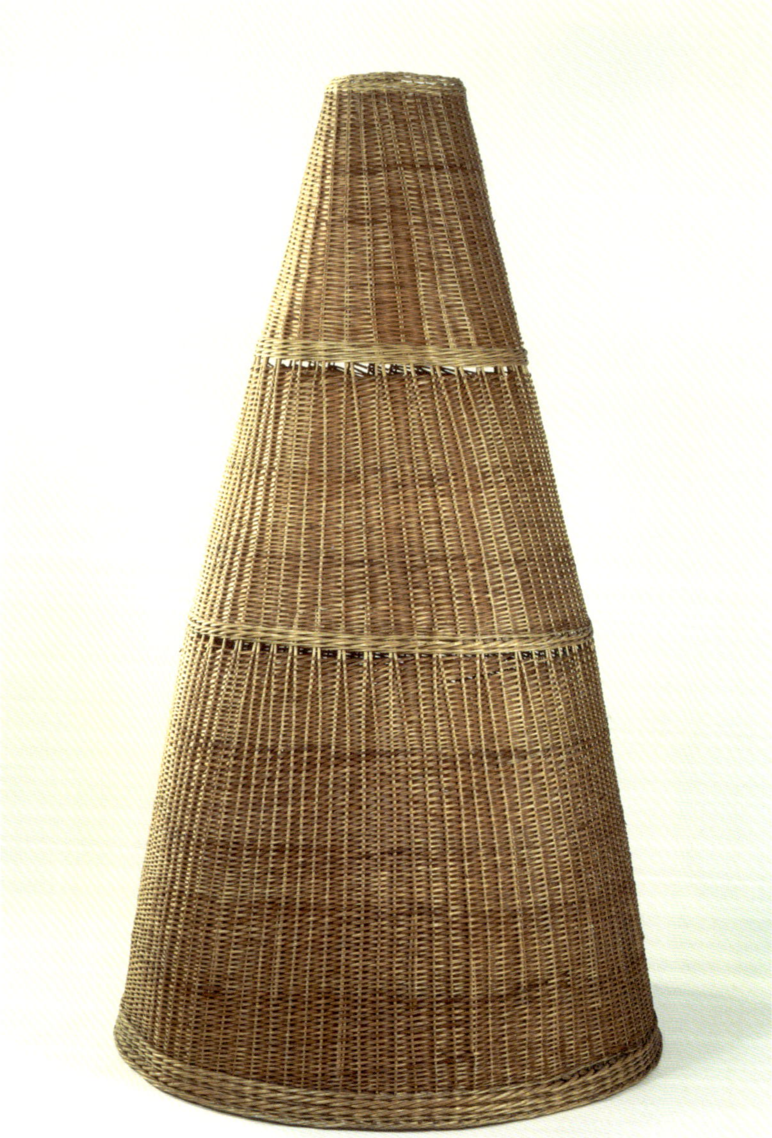

metal tubing with stucco, a material used in building, wrapped around the upper part shaped into a flattened coil. This exhibition at Galleria L'Attico was the first time Merz made works within the gallery, rather than in his studio.

'*Cono*' ('Cone', *c.*1967) [Cat. 3], a sculpture with a somewhat obscured exhibition history,[24] likewise emphasises process. Standing just over two metres tall, '*Cono*' is formed from willow by craftsmen. It is seemingly functional, but is at a scale too large for any clear use. In the exhibition catalogue for the three-day exhibition-event *Arte povera + azione povera*, the 'cone' is described as sitting on top of a pot of boiling beans, the heat causing steam to rise through the top.[25] Like the igloo forms that Merz would begin to develop in 1968, '*Cono*' is human-sized, suggesting shelter and portability. The first of Merz's igloo forms was '*Igloo di Giap*' ('Giap's igloo', 1968), made of sandbags inscribed in neon with the statement: 'If the enemy concentrates, he loses ground; if he scatters, he loses force' written, like the aforementioned *Che fare?,* in continuous neon, the text in Italian. Merz describes the words as taken from the Vietcong General Vo Nguyen Giap,[26] pointing to the anti-Vietnam War protests and the civil disobedience that spread across Italy as the country struggled: in 1966 500,000 construction workers went out on strike, and in 1968 mass demonstrations against the Vietnam War took place across Turin. Like the blankets, bottles and neon, proclamations of resistance in this context were as commonplace as any other of his materials. Merz, though, stated that he was wary of such a reading: 'I wanted to avoid analysing situations in terms of slogans which diminish things to social positives or negatives, like saying I prefer communists, liberals etc.'[27] The statements he chose are ambiguous, requiring application rather than being knee-jerk rhetoric. In this exhibition an overtly political testament is displayed high on the wall in the central gallery. '*Sciopero generale azione politica relativa proclamata relativamente all'arte*' ('General strike political action relative proclaimed relatively to art', 1970) [Cat. 12] uses a rounded capital typeface, rather than writing based on the artist's own hand, an exception to Merz's approach to neon light writing. Usually he

24 See *The Tate Gallery 1982–94: Illustrated Catalogue of Acquisitions*, London, 1986 which notes that there is some confusion over the dating and exhibition history of this work.

25 1968, Amalfi, Arsenale, organised by Marcello Rumma and Germano Celant.

26 It is actually a paraphrase from Sun Zu's *The Art of War*, written around 500 BC and widely read in the 1960s.

27 Tisdall, Caroline, interview with Mario Merz in London, September 1975, *Studio International*, January/February 1976, pp. 11–17.

12

Mario Merz

Sciopero generale azione politica relativa proclamata relativamente all'arte

(General strike political action relative proclaimed relatively to art, 1970)

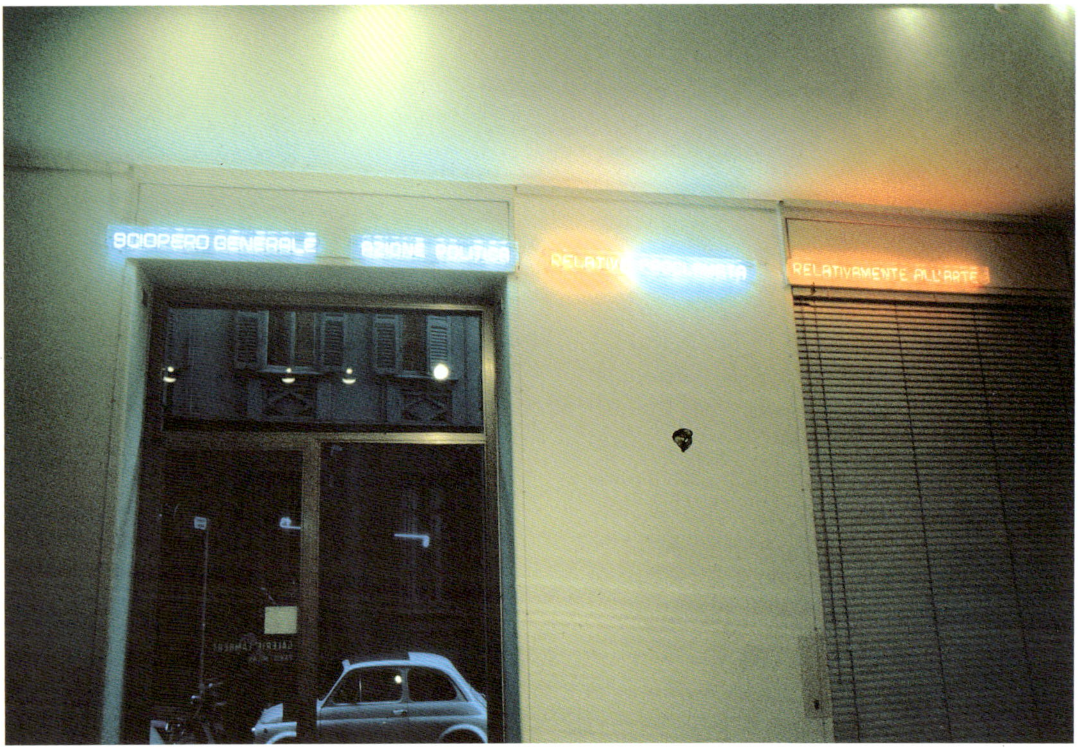

chooses clear neon, which appears blue, or tubing painted white – here red is used. The words of the title are paired into Perspex boxes – the first two in white neon, the third white and red, and the final pair red – making a rhythmic call for activism in the face of artistic practice, pointing to Merz's formative political engagements that framed his work made in the period this exhibition studies. The overt collapse of politics into art is perhaps why the artist used this distinct formula. His was not a practice based on formal materialism that sought to remove art from the world.

'*Igloo di Giap*', like all the igloo forms, operates as an open and closed space. Merz described his hemispheres, that became a signature form, as the simplest way to evaluate three-dimensional space, a 'border zone between full and empty; a field of complementary tensions where forces of meeting and collision are engaged'.[28] In the gallery the igloo becomes an articulator of space, operating simultaneously inside and outside, sitting firmly on the curvature of the earth that is hidden by the micro scale of the floor – a conceit that fascinated Merz.[29] In this exhibition two igloos are displayed. '*Objet cache-toi*' ('Object hide yourself', 1968) [Cat. 5] is an armature of bars and wire netting surrounded by linen bags, filled with wood shavings, around which the title wraps. The title recalls '*Cono*'s hidden beans, as well as the legacies of Duchamp's hidden objects.[30] As with Giap's statement, the demand 'object hide yourself' is tautological, asking that the object retreats from its own form. By distinction '*Igloo Fibonacci (Fibonacci unit)*' (1970) [Cat. 9] is an open igloo, a frame made from brass tubing and steel hinges, eight legs standing on numbered marble discs. In 1970 Merz began to use the Fibonacci series intensively, describing, in 1971, this naturally observed formula as:

> … published in Pisa in 1202, it is a very simple idea. Each number adds up with or involves the preceding number in the formation of the following one, e.g. 1 + 0 + 1. Then one adds up with one to form two. And two adds up with one to form three.[31]

28 Celant, Germano, 'Mario Merz: The Artist as Nomad', *Artforum*, December 1979, p. 53.

29 See Petrovsky, Hugo, 'On Arte Povera and Mario Merz' in *Mario Merz*, exh. cat., Fundación Proa, Buenos Aires, 2003, p. 106.

30 See Marcel Duchamp's 'With Hidden Noise' (1916) and Robert Morris' 'Box with the Sound of its Own Making' (1961), both discussed in Penelope Curtis (ed.) *With Hidden Noise: Sculpture, Video and Ventriloquism*, exh. cat., Henry Moore Institute, Leeds, 2004.

31 'Mario Merz: The Fibonacccia' (1971) cited in Carolyn Christov-Bakargiev (ed.) *Arte Povera*, Phaidon, 1999, p. 252.

9

Mario Merz

Igloo Fibonacci (Fibonacci unit)

(Fibonacci Igloo (Fibonacci unit), 1970)

11

Mario Merz, Lumaca

(Mario Merz, Snail, 1970)

From

Gerry Schum (1938–73)

Identifications

1970

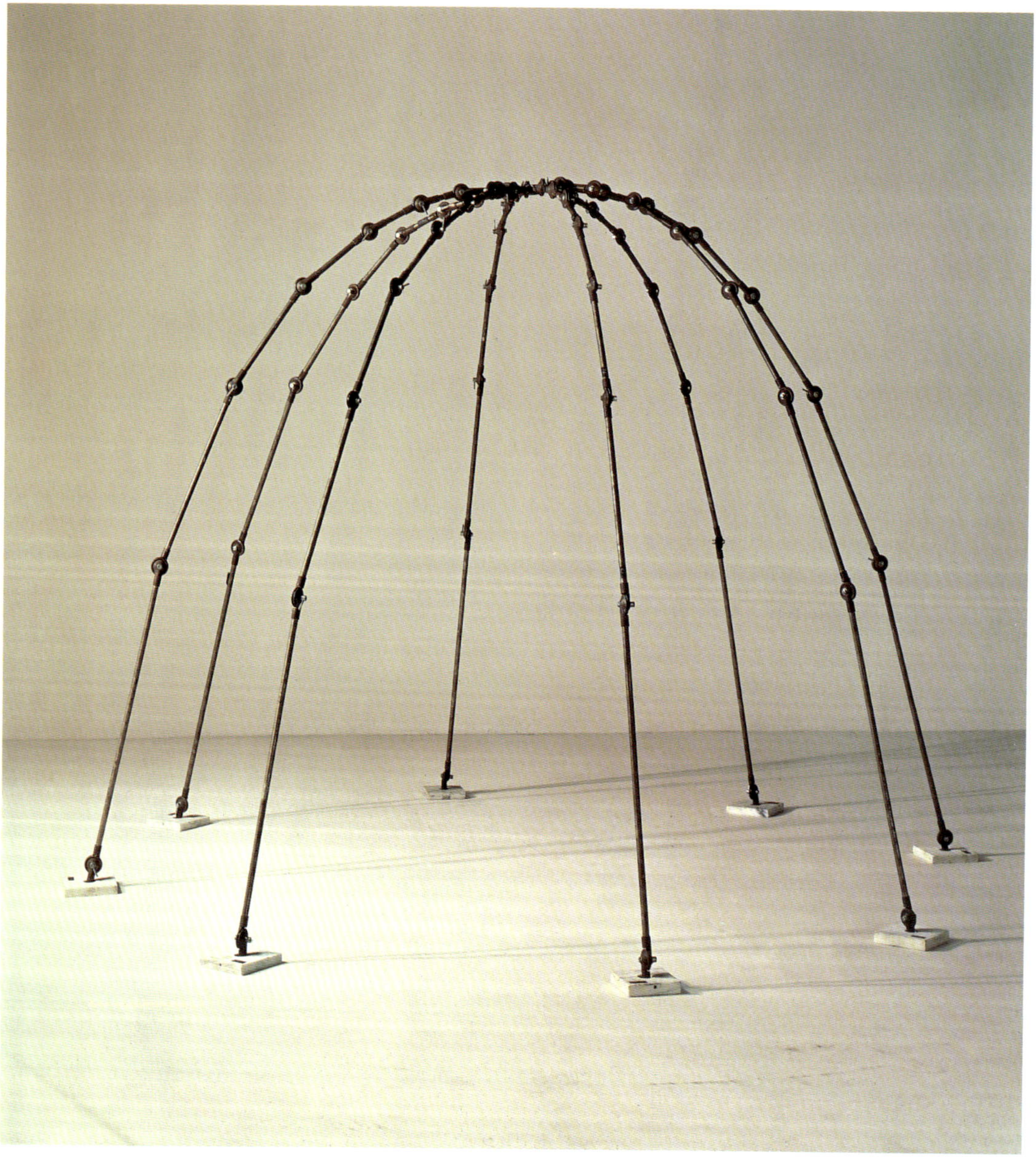

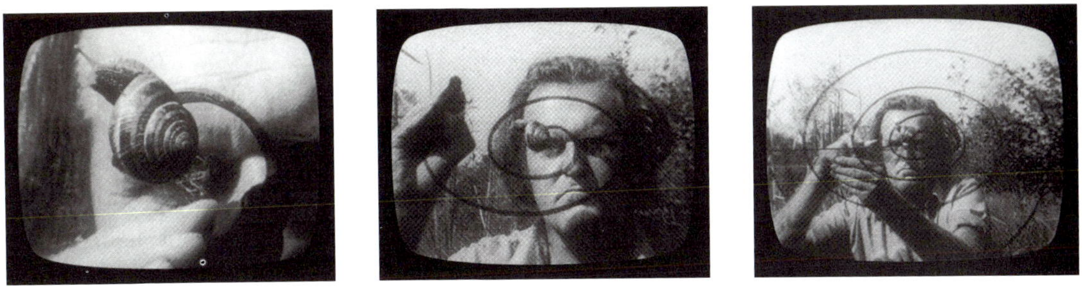

In 1970 Merz worked with Gerry Schum on an exhibition that took the form of two television programmes,[32] with the one minute twenty second black and white film *Lumaca* (*Snail*, 1970) [Cat. 11]. A snail sits on a sheet of glass, behind which Merz is seen in the landscape explaining the Fibonacci series, aided by drawing spirals around the snail on the glass. The partner to the moving image work is '*Fibonacci spirale*' ('Fibonacci spiral', 1970) [Cat. 10], a sculpture formed from a Plexiglas box holding a copy of Schum's film, the surface annotated with the note that this is a 'video-sculpture' with the Fibonacci sequence from one to five marked to the left hand side of the box. Merz was interested in this mathematical series because of its infinite possibilities where every move to the future is sustained by the past. The sequence was first observed by the mathematician and nomad cleric Leonardo de Pisa who observed spiral forms of growth in naturally occurring patterns of multiplication, such as snail shells, pinecones and the reproduction of bees and rabbits. Observation is a central tenet in Merz's work: his sculptures use what is ready at hand to observe, rather than explain, the habits and forms that make up our surroundings. Although Merz employed numbers as a sculptural medium from 1970, his interest in number proliferation was hinted at in 1968 in Giap's numerical formula for occupying space and when he looked at patterns of natural growth in the sculptures '*Cere*' ('Wax'). In these a canvas was set between two tree branches through which Merz had observed light falling. Liquid wax was poured in the space; by the next day it had hardened, leaving a sculpture formed by measurement.

In 1970 Merz experimented with the sequence in a variety of ways. As well as making *Lumaca* he worked with a violinist on the occasion of the third *Biennale internazionale della giovane pittura* at the Museum Civico in Bologna to sound out the progression;[33] built the sequence around two historic paintings in the exhibition, *Amore mio* at Palazzo Ricci, Montepulciano;[34] and in *Processi di pensiero visualizzati*[35] at the Kunstmuseum Lucerne annotated a series of leaning planes of glass. In this latter example, '*Seri Fibonacci*' ('Fibonacci Series'), the glass surfaces were

32 Titled *Identifications*, it was broadcast in Baden Baden, Germany on the Sudwestfunk channel.

33 Curated by Renato Bailli, Maurizio Calvesi, Andrea Emiliano and Tomasso Trini.

34 Curated by Achille Bonito Oliva.

35 Curated by Jean-Christophe Ammann.

13

Mario Merz

Appoggiata alla testa, appoggiata al convesso, appoggiata al concavo, appoggiata al muro, appoggiata alla casa, appoggiata al cervello

(Propped at the head, propped at the convex, propped at the concave, propped at the wall, propped at the house, propped at the brain, 1977)

10

Mario Merz

Fibonacci spirale

(Fibonacci spiral, 1970)

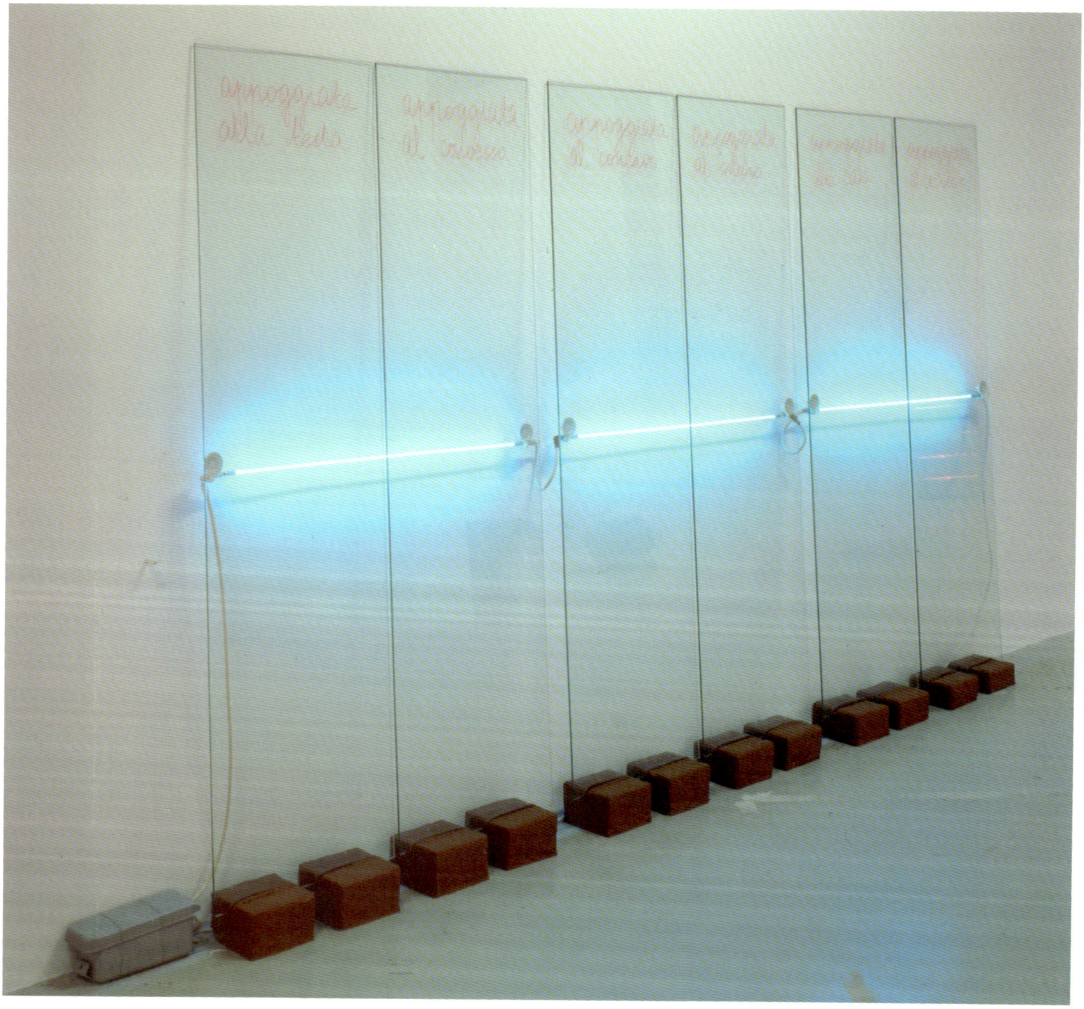

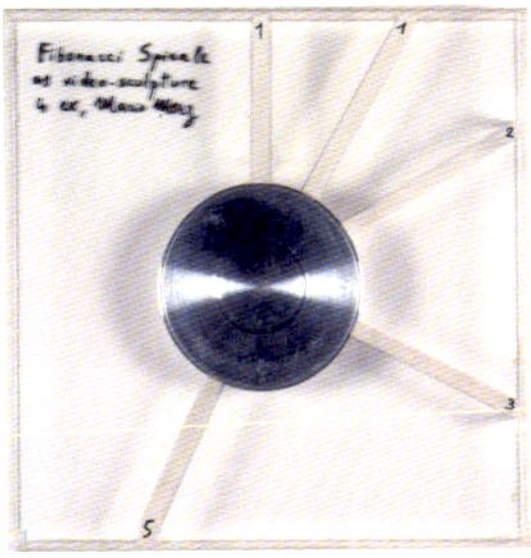

traversed by neon and numbered by hand according to the sequence. Potentially, the glass panes could be extended into infinity.

'Appoggiata alla testa, appoggiata al convesso, appoggiata al concavo, appoggiata al muro, appoggiata alla casa, appoggiata al cervello' ('Propped at the head, propped at the convex, propped at the concave, propped at the wall, propped at the house, propped at the brain', 1977) [Cat. 13], the latest work in *Mario Merz: What Is to Be Done?*, likewise uses leaning planes of glass. As with all the works under consideration here, *'Appoggiata'* is indicative of a constant return and extension that characterises Merz's artistic practice – it is a continuous proliferation. *'Bottiglia'*, for example, is one of a number of experiments using a bottle and neon and, as discussed above, *'Che fare?'* was posed in a number of ways. In the 1969 Galleria L'Attico exhibition a work made of glass and clay titled *'Vetri appoggiati'* ('Propped Glass') was exhibited; and in Harald Szeeman's exhibition *When Attitudes Become Form* of the same year a work titled *'Appoggiati'* made of glass and mastic was made on site at Kunsthalle Berne. This *'Appoggiati'*, like *'Sciopero generale'* and the glass stacked on the roof rack of *'Automobile trapassata dal neon'*, consists of pairs, the glass companions linked with a strip of neon held in place by hooks and suckers on the reverse of the glass. As with *'Sciopero generale'*, the text is written in red. Each leans against the wall, holding a statement announcing different ways to lean; each textual 'threat' written in red handwriting directly on the glass, concerned with relationships between space and its perception. The work uses the architecture of the Henry Moore Institute's walls to support itself, becoming anchored to the space and claiming the surrounds as its own. This strategy is also used in *'Torciglione'* ('Helicoil', 1969) [Cat. 8], a work that precedes the use of the Fibonacci series. Also propped against the wall, this earlier work is displayed here in the same gallery as *'Cono'*, *'Appoggiata'*, *'Automobile trapassata dal neon'* and *'Sciopero generale'*, the stucco flattened into a coil around the pole, its mathematical equivalent the cone rather than the spiral.

8

Mario Merz

Torciglione

(Helicoil, 1969)

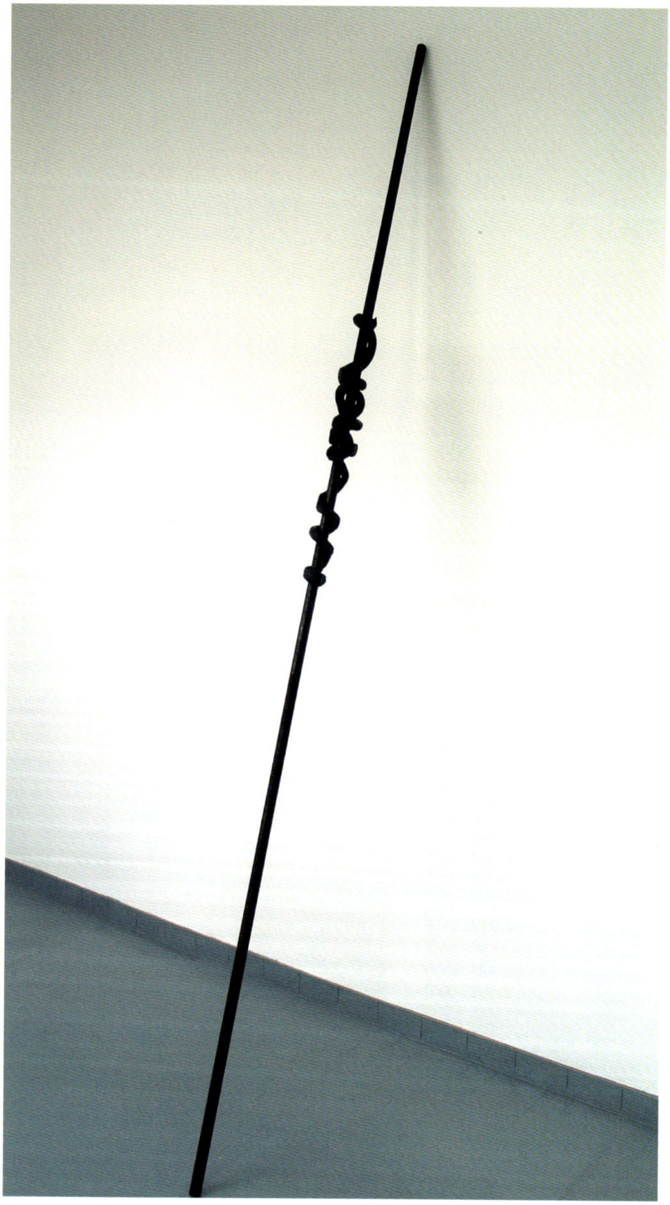

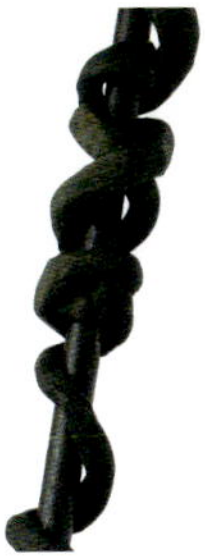

As an accompaniment to *Mario Merz: What Is to Be Done?*, Tacita Dean's 16mm film *Mario Merz* (2002) [Cat. 14] is displayed at the Institute. This is a study of the ageing Merz observed by Dean in Tuscany, sitting in silence with a large pinecone in his hand. It is ostensibly a portrait, but more importantly a study of light in space and form in nature – central concerns in Merz's sculptural investigations. Dean describes how she was invited to undertake a project in Tuscany, where:

> Marisa Merz was invited too. Those who knew Mario and Marisa Merz understood that if you invited one artist, you got both [...] When eventually I asked: 'Mario, can I film you?' he replied 'Yes, but no speaking' and immediately sat himself on a chair under a tree, cupping a large pinecone in his lap. His choice of prop was generated by his sculptor's interest in the Fibonacci sequence and its instances in nature.[36]

Importantly for Merz, the Fibonacci series is 'not a multiplication, but the proliferation of a single unit'.[37] Numbers provide a means of observation, rather than accumulation; they are abstract inventions that only become concrete once applied. The Fibonacci sequence is a system that releases numbers from the demand to perform a productive function, with the numbers proliferating in a process that unfolds over time. This was Merz's approach to art making: he was concerned with observation, making objects of and in the world. His was a commitment to presenting rather than representing, utilising sculpture to undo structures of perception.

Lisa Le Feuvre
HEAD OF SCULPTURE STUDIES
HENRY MOORE INSTITUTE
JULY 2011

36 Dean, Tacita, Mario Merz Obituary in the *Guardian*, November 13 2003.

37 Tisdall, Caroline, interview with Mario Merz in London, September 1975, *Studio International*, January/February 1976, pp. 11–17.

List of works

1

Salamino

(Small Salami, 1966)

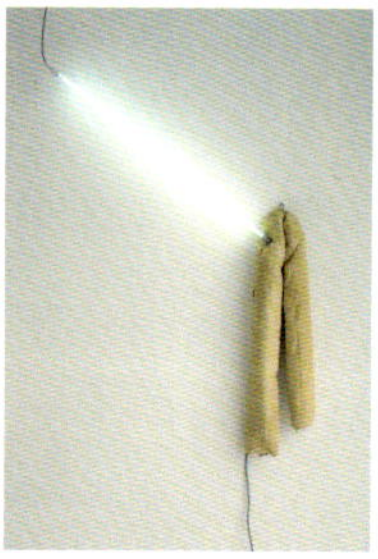

Fabric, neon tube, transformer
254 × 90 × 70 cm
Collection Fundação de Serralves – Museu de Arte Contemporânea, Porto

SELECTED EXHIBITION HISTORY

Mario Merz
Solomon R. Guggenheim Museum, New York, 1989
Voici : 100 ans d'art contemporain
Palais des Beaux-Arts, Brussels, 2000
Antagonismes. Casos d'estudi
MACBA, Barcelona, 2001
Brossa i el seu temps
Fundació Vila Casas, Barcelona, 2002
Mario Merz
Galleria Civica d'Arte Moderna e Contemporanea, Turin, 2005
Arte Pobre na Colecção da Fundação de Serralves
Pavilhão Centro de Portugal, Coimbra, 2005

2

Bottiglia

(Bottle, 1967)

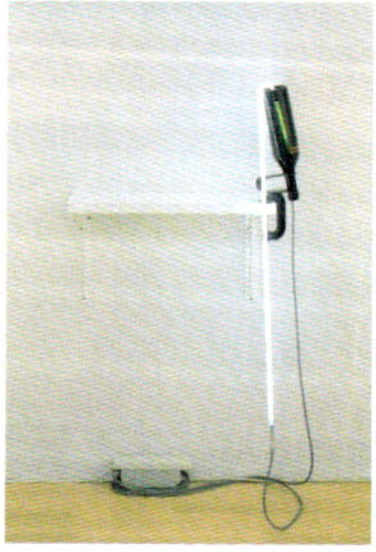

Neon, wine bottle, clamp, shelf, transformer
Display dimensions variable
Sammlung Goetz, Munich

SELECTED EXHIBITION HISTORY

Arte Povera. Arbeiten und Dokumente aus der Sammlung Goetz 1958 bis heute. Teil I
Sammlung Goetz, Munich, 1999
Mario Merz
Galleria Civica d'Arte Moderna e Contemporanea, Castello di Rivoli – Museo d'Arte Contemporanea and Fondazione Merz, Turin, 2005

3

Cono

(Cone, *c.*1967)

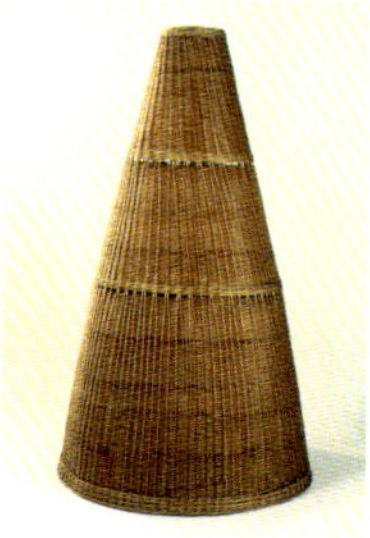

Wood (willow)
221 × 129.5 × 129.5 cm
Tate, purchased 1983
T03674

SELECTED EXHIBITION HISTORY

Mario Merz, Important works 1966–83
Anthony d'Offay Gallery, London, 1983
Ergo, material. Arte povera
Museo Universitario Arte Contemporáneo, Mexico City, 2010
Basketry: Making Human Nature
Sainsbury Centre for the Visual Arts, Norwich, 2011

4

Che fare?

(What is to be done? After 1967)

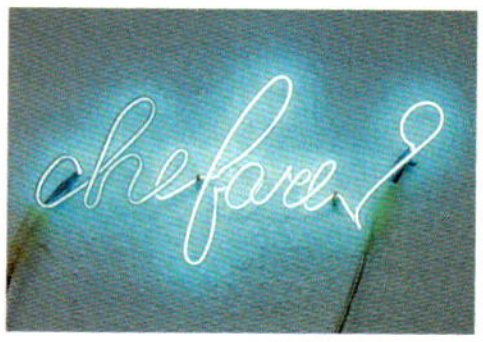

Neon lettering, transformer
25 × 45 cm

Staatliche Museen zu Berlin, Nationalgalerie, Sammlung Marzona
Copy from NG/MZ 95/02

SELECTED EXHIBITION HISTORY
Das 20. Jahrhundert in der Neuen Nationalgalerie – Gegenwelten
Neue Nationalgalerie, Berlin, 2005

Mario Merz
Castello di Rivoli – Museo d'Arte Contemporanea, Turin, 2004
ArchiSculpture: Dialogues between Architecture and Sculpture from the 18th century to the Present Day
Museo Guggenheim, Bilbao, 2005 and Kunstmuseum Wolfsburg, 2006
1968. Die große Unschuld
Kunsthalle Bielefeld, 2009

5
Objet cache-toi
(Object hide yourself, 1968)

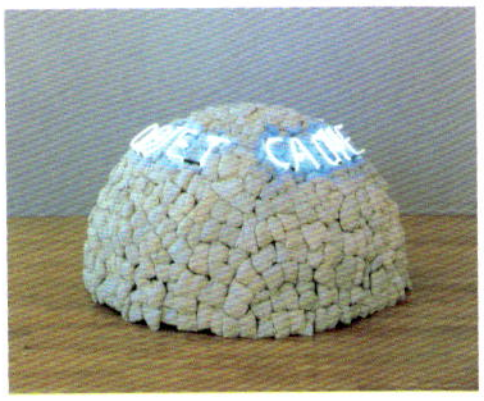

Iron rods, wire mesh, linen sacks filled with wood-wool, neon tubing, transformers
110 × 210 cm
Kunstmuseum Wolfsburg
1997/01

SELECTED EXHIBITION HISTORY
Prospect '68
Kunsthalle Düsseldorf, 1968
Galerie Ileana Sonnabend, Paris, 1969
Colección Sonnabend. 25 años de selección y actividad
Museo Nacional Centro de Arte Reina Sofia, Madrid, 1988
25 années de choix et d'activités d'Ileana et Michael Sonnabend
CAPC Musée d'art contemporain de Bordeaux, 1988
La Collezione Sonnabend: dalla pop art in poi
Galleria Nazionale d'Arte Moderna, Rome, 1989
Mario Merz
Solomon R. Guggenheim Museum, New York, 1989
Sammlung Ileana Sonnabend
Deichtorhallen, Hamburg and Kunsthalle der Hypo-Kulturstiftung, Munich, 1996

6
Che fare?
(What is to be done? 1968–73)

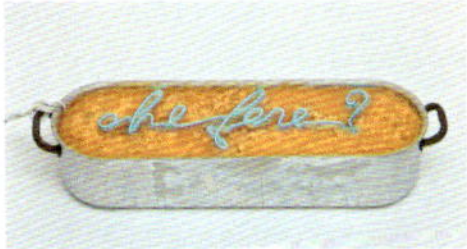

Aluminium, wax, neon, transformer
12.5 × 66.8 × 19.1 cm
ARTIST ROOMS Tate and National Galleries of Scotland
Acquired jointly through The d'Offay Donation with assistance from the National Heritage Memorial Fund and the Art Fund 2008
AR00598

7
Automobile trapassata dal neon
(Automobile pierced by neon, 1969/1982)

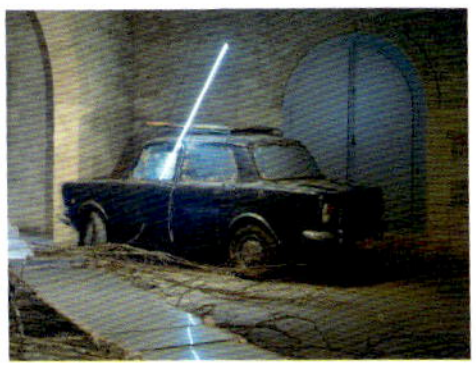

Simca 1000, metal, glass, wax, clay, neon, transformer
320 × 380 × 147 cm
Collection du CAPC Musée d'art contemporain de Bordeaux
1989–04(2)

Installation view of the exhibition *Christian Boltanski, Daniel Buren, Gilbert & George, Jannis Kounellis, Sol LeWitt, Richard Long, Mario Merz*, CAPC Musée d'art contemporain de Bordeaux, 1990 showing detail of Mario Merz, 'Che fare?', 1969/1990

SELECTED EXHIBITION HISTORY

Che fare?
Galleria L'Attico, Rome, 1969
Arte Povera, Antiform: Sculptures, 1966–1969
CAPC, Entrepôt Lainé, Bordeaux, 1982
Christian Boltanski, Daniel Buren, Gilbert & George, Jannis Kounellis, Sol LeWitt, Richard Long, Mario Merz
CAPC Musée d'art contemporain de Bordeaux, 1990
Arca de Noé
Fundação de Serralves – Museu de Arte Contemporânea, Porto, 1994
Les années 70: l'art en cause
CAPC Musée d'art contemporain de Bordeaux, 2002

8
Torciglione

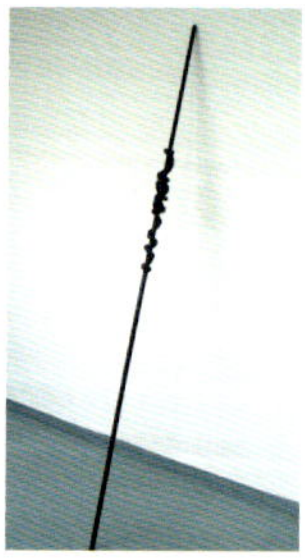

(Helicoil, 1969)

Iron rod, resin
h. 283 cm
Private collection

SELECTED EXHIBITION HISTORY

Che fare?
Galleria L'Attico, Rome, 1969

9
Igloo Fibonacci (Fibonacci unit)

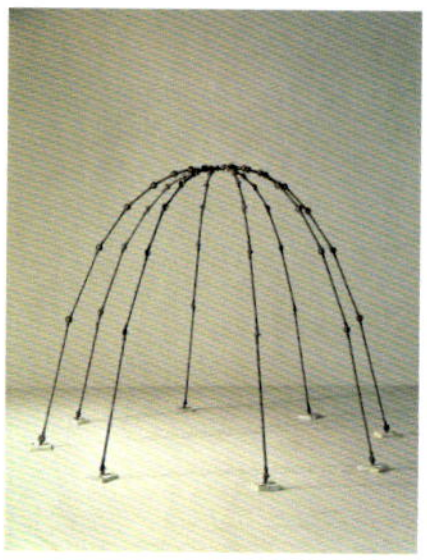

(Fibonacci igloo (Fibonacci unit), 1970)

Brass pipes, steel hinge, eight marble slabs with adhesive tape and white numbers
180 × 260 cm
Kunstmuseum Wolfsburg
1997/02

SELECTED EXHIBITION HISTORY

Ileana Sonnabend Gallery, New York, 1970
Processi di pensiero visualizzati
Kunstmuseum Luzern, 1970
Mario Merz
Museum Folkwang, Essen, 1979
Concetto-Imago: Generationswechsel in Italien
Kunstverein Bonn, 1983
Mario Merz
Kunsthaus Zürich, 1985
Colección Sonnabend. 25 años de selección y actividad
Museo Nacional Centro de Arte Reina Sofia, Madrid, 1987
25 années de choix et d'activités d'Ileana et Michael Sonnabend
CAPC Musée d'art contemporain de Bordeaux, 1988
Mario Merz
Solomon R. Guggenheim Museum, New York, 1989
La Collezione Sonnabend: dalla pop art in poi
Galleria Nazionale d'Arte Moderna, Rome, 1989
Gravity and Grace. The Changing Condition of Sculpture 1965–75
Hayward Gallery, London, 1993

Même si c'est la nuit
CAPC Musée d'art contemporain de Bordeaux, 1994
Zero to Infinity: Arte Povera 1962–1972
Tate Modern, London, 2001
ArchiSkulptur: Dialoge zwischen Architektur und Plastik vom 18. Jahrhundert bis heute
Kunstmuseum Wolfsburg, 2006
Philip Taaffe. Das Leben der Formen. Werke 1980–2008
Kunstmuseum Wolfsburg, 2008
Dopplereffekt. Bilder in Kunst und Wissenschaft
Kunsthalle zu Kiel, 2010

10
Fibonacci spirale
(Fibonacci spiral, 1970)

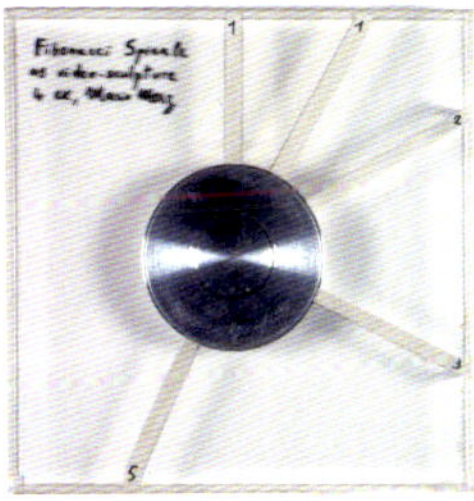

Plexiglas, aluminium
35 × 35 × 5 cm
Staatliche Museen zu Berlin, Nationalgalerie, Sammlung Marzona
NG/MZ 0613

SELECTED EXHIBITION HISTORY
Circle Sphere Cosmos
Kunsthalle Würth, Schwäbish Hall, 2007

11
Mario Merz, Lumaca
(Mario Merz, Snail, 1970)

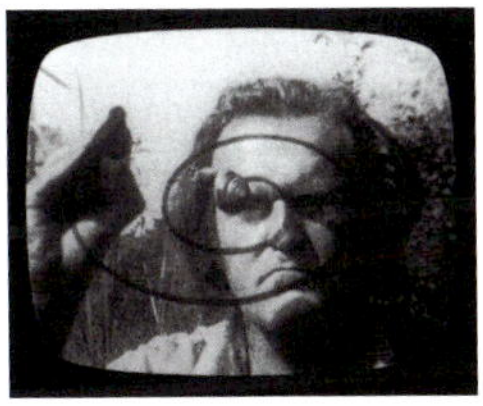

From
Gerry Schum (1938–73)
Identifications
1970
16 mm film, b&w, soundtrack, 36 minutes
DVD, b&w, soundtrack, 1 minute 30 seconds
Staatliche Museen zu Berlin, Kunstbibliothek, Sammlung Marzona
Exhibition copy

12
Sciopero generale azione politica relativa proclamata relativamente all'arte
(General strike political action relative proclaimed relatively to art, 1970)

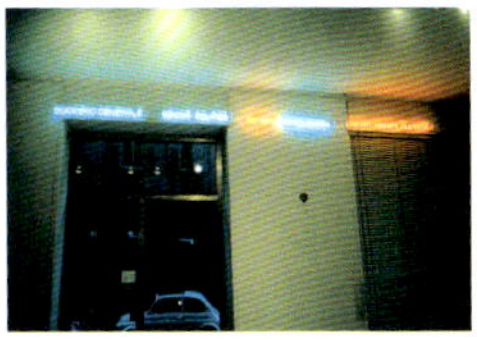

Plexiglas, neon, transformers
10 × 535 × 10 cm
Fondazione Merz, Turin
120/1970/NN

SELECTED EXHIBITION HISTORY
Galleria Françoise Lambert, Milan, 1970

13
Appoggiata alla testa, appoggiata al convesso, appoggiata al concavo, appoggiata al muro, appoggiata alla casa, appoggiata al cervello
(Propped at the head, propped at the convex, propped at the concave, propped at the wall, propped at the house, propped at the brain, 1977)

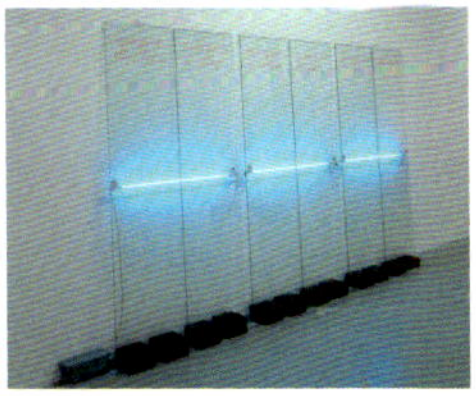

Glass, neon, suction cups, transformer
185 × 435 cm
Collection de l'Institut d'art contemporain, Rhône-Alpes
85.171

SELECTED EXHIBITION HISTORY

20 oeuvres de la collection Rhône-Alpes
Centre d'art contemporain, Geneva, 1985
Mario Merz, Giovanni Anselmo
Ecole municipale d'arts plastiques, Mâcon, 1986
Collection souvenir
Nouveau Musée, Villeurbanne, 1976
Uno sguardo, un regard de Bruno Corà sur les oeuvres du Frac Rhône-Alpes. Un regard, uno sguardo di Bruno Corà sulle opere del Frac Rhone-Alpes
Centre national d'art contemporain, Grenoble, 1986 and Académie des Beaux-Arts, Naples, 1987
Oeuvres du Frac Rhône-Alpes
Centre culturel de Flaine, Magland, 1987
Turin 1965–1987. De l'Arte Povera dans les collections publiques françaises
Musée Savoisien, Chambéry, Musée de l'Hospice Comtesse, Lille, Musée municipal, La Roche-sur-Yon, 1987
Générations...
Musée Hébert, La Tronche, 1988
L'inventaire
Manufrance, Saint-Etienne, 1988
Vision sur l'art contemporain. Oeuvres du Frac Rhône-Alpes
Galerie l'Encan, Louvain, 1988
Sculptures sur la ville
Musée-Château, Annecy, 1993
Ensayo general (Répétition générale)
Museo de Arte Carrillo Gill Insitituto nacional de bellas artes, Mexico, Bibliothèque Luis-Angel Arango Casa de Exposiciones, Bogota, Museo de Arte Contemporaneo, Santiago, Museo Nacional de Bellas Artes, Buenos Aires, 1995–6
Lumière !
Mairie, Roanne, 2000
Sculpture contemporaine
Subsistances, Lyon, 2001
Trésors publics / Esprit des lieux
Palais des Papes, Avignon, 2003
Fins des histoires ? Une traversée plurielle dans la collection Frac Rhône-Alpes
Musée des Beaux-Arts Musées d'art et d'histoire, Chambéry, 2003
Collection de l'Institut d'art contemporain
Mairie, Grignan, 2004
Le plaisir au dessin
Musée des Beaux-Arts, Lyon, 2007
Locus oculi par Bernhard Rüdiger
Avec les oeuvres des collections de l'Institut d'art contemporain, Villeurbanne et du Musée d'art moderne de Saint-Etienne Métropole
Château de la Bâtie d'Urfé, 2009

14

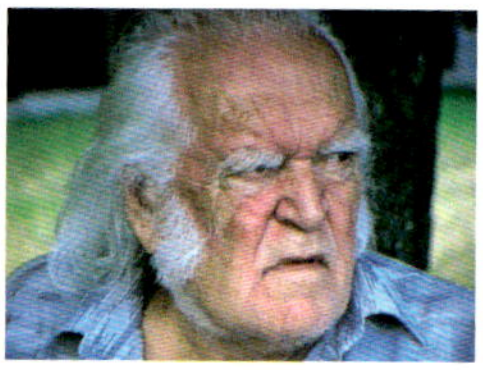

Tacita Dean (b. 1965)
Mario Merz
2002

16 mm film, colour, optical sound,
8 minutes 30 seconds
Edition of 4
Frith Street Gallery, London

SELECTED EXHIBITION HISTORY

Arte all'Arte VII, San Gimignano, 2002
Kunstverein für die Rheinlande und Westfalen, 2002
Venice Biennale 2003
Frith Street Gallery, 2004
Body: New Work from the UK
Vancouver Art Gallery and 4 other venues in Canada, 2005

The essays form a collection of occasional writings on sculpture, in some cases accompanying exhibitions, and usually embodying a personal – even political – point of view. They also respond to fellowships and to the Leeds collections.

Annotated titles are now out of print. Reference copies are available in the Henry Moore Institute Research Library, or on-line at: www.henry-moore.org/hmi-journal/homepage

Essays can be purchased from the Institute bookshop or from our website: www.henry-moore.org/hmf/shop/hmi-essays

For subscription information, contact publications@henry-moore.org

*1 *Medardo Rosso's Italian Background*
Sandra Beresford 1994

*2 *Art and Spatial Politics*
Deanna Petherbridge 1994

*3 *Reproduction in Sculpture: Dilution or Increase?*
Ed Allington and Ben Dhaliwal 1994

*4 *Public Art Commissions, Exemplified by Auke de Vries*
Franz W Kaiser 1995

5 *The Very Impress of the Object: Photographing Sculpture from Fox Talbot to the Present Day*
Geraldine Johnson 1995 30 b&w illustrations £2.00
ISBN 1 900081 10 5

*6 *William Tucker: The Language of a Sculptor*
Alison Sleeman 1995

*7 *Paule Vézelay/Hans Arp: The Enchantments of Purity*
Sarah Wilson 1995

*8 *Gabo's Stones*
Martin Hammer and Christina Lodder 1995

*9 *Bernard Meadows*
Penelope Curtis 1995

10 *Quatremère de Quincy's Role in the Revival of Polychromy in Sculpture*
Yvonne Luke 1996 14 b&w illustrations £2.00
ISBN 1 900081 16 4

11 *On Artistic Knowledge: Notes for a Minor Platonic Exercise*
Jyrki Siukonen 1996 6 b&w illustrations £2.00
ISBN 1 900081 70 9

12 *Duel: Tracy Mackenna & Karla Sachse*
Kerstin May 1996 8 b&w illustrations £2.00
ISBN 1 900081 85 7

13 *Sleep in Sculpture: Babies from the Bowes*
Briony Fer, Fiona Russell, Alison Yarrington 1996 4 b&w illustrations £2.00 ISBN 1 900081 80 6

14 *Peter Scheemakers: The Famous Statuary 1691-1781*
Ingrid Roscoe 1996 12pp 24 b&w illustrations £2.00 ISBN 1 900081 11 3

*15 *More and Less: The Early Works of Richard Long*
Alison Sleeman 1997

16 *Michael Kidner: Making Maps, Looking for Landmarks*
Interviewed by Penelope Curtis, edited by Dorcas Taylor 1997 5 b&w illustrations £2.00
ISBN 1 900081 46 6

17 *Chromaphobia: Ancient and Modern, and a Few Notable Exceptions*
David Batchelor 1997 12 b&w illustrations £2.00
ISBN 1 900081 26 1

18 *Eric Gill in Yorkshire*
Graham Carey 1997 12pp 23 b&w illustrations
£2.00 ISBN 1 900081 66 0

19 *Rodin: Rhythm and Ritual*
Stephen Feeke and Ramsay Burt 1998
9 b&w illustrations £2.00 ISBN 1 900081 76 8

20 *Peter Shelton: Soul Soundings*
Jacquelynn Baas 1997 16pp 23 b&w illustrations
£2.00 ISBN 1 900081 61 X

21 *Work and the Image: The Image of the Worker in the Work of the Sculptor*
Terry Friedman, Fiona Russell, Dorcas Taylor 1998
8 b&w illustrations £2.00 ISBN 1 900081 71 7

22 *The Space of the Page: Sequence, Continuity and Material*
John Janssen 1997 16pp 11 b&w illustrations £2.00
ISBN 1 900081 56 3

23 *Gilbert Bayes (1872-1953): From Arts and Crafts to the Light Monumental*
Philip Ward-Jackson 1998 23 b&w illustrations
£2.00 ISBN 1 900081 81 4

24 *Sampled: The Use of Fabric in Sculpture*
Gerard Williams, Gill Nicol, Fiona Russell 1999
21 b&w illustrations £2.00 ISBN 1 900081 22 9

25 *Frederick Thrupp (1812-1895): Survivals from a Sculptor's Studio*
Martin Greenwood 1999 17 b&w illustrations
£2.00 ISBN 1 900081 91 1

26 *The Encounter and The Struggle: Lipchitz Maquettes 1928-1942*
Cathy Pütz 1999 13 b&w illustrations £2.00
ISBN 1 900081 02 4

27 *Etienne Martin*
Interviewed by Irmeline Lebeer 2000
1 b&w illustration £2.00 ISBN 1 900081 42 3

28 *Sculpture in Literature*
Mary Hamer, Anthony Hughes, Peter Read 2000
2 b&w illustrations £2.00 ISBN 1 900081 57 1

29 *Attending to the Barely Made*
Jacqui Poncelet interviewed by Penelope Curtis
2000 17 b&w illustrations £2.00
ISBN 1 900081 62 8

30 *Ornament as Sculpture: The Sam Wilson Chimneypiece in Leeds City Art Gallery*
Martina Droth 2000 10 b&w illustrations £2.00
ISBN 1 900081 72 5

31 *The Cult of the Statuette In Late Victorian Britain*
Martina Droth, Jason Edwards, David J Getsy,
Matthew Withey 2000 10pp 13 b&w illustrations
£2.00 ISBN 1 900081 77 6

32 *Le Corbusier – Savina*
Christopher Green 2001 12 b&w illustrations £2.00
ISBN 1 900081 92 X

33 *Things to Come: Eric Kennington's War God*
Sue Malvern 2001 12pp 10 b&w illustrations £2.00
ISBN 1 900081 13 X

34 *Enchanted Monuments: Inside and Outside Jean Dubuffet*
John Gibson 2001 12 b&w illustrations £2.00
ISBN 1 900081 33 4

35 *The Conquest of Space: On the Prevalence of Maps in Contemporary Art*
Deborah Schultz 2001 12 b&w illustrations £2.00
ISBN 1 900081 38 5

36 *Shine: Sculpture and Surface in the 1920s and 1930s*
Introduction by Jon Wood 2002 24pp
20 b&w illustrations £2.00 ISBN 1 900081 48 2

37 *Model Forms: Sculpture/Architecture in 50s & 60s' Britain*
Steven Gartside 2002 40pp 115 × 165mm
10 illustrations (8 colour) £2.00 ISBN 1 900081 78 4

38 *Gaston Lachaise and 'Elevation' 1912-27*
Jon Wood 2003 12pp 11 b&w illustrations £2.00
ISBN 1 900081 83 0

39 *A Fine Tomorrow: Sculpture and Socialism in mid-century Britain*
Matthew Withey 2003 12pp 13 b&w illustrations
£2.00 ISBN 1 900081 93 8

40 *A Context of Commitment: The Sculpture of Betty Rea*
Gillian Whiteley 2003 12pp 10 b&w illustrations
£2.00 ISBN 1 900081 09 1

41 *Refashioning the Figure: The Sketchbooks of Archipenko*
Marek Bartelik 2003 12pp 12 b&w illustrations
£2.00 ISBN 1 900081 14 8

42 *Making History: Edinburgh 1845*
Rocco Lieuallen, Matthew Withey 2003 16pp
15 b&w illustrations £2.00 ISBN 1 900081 19 9

43 *Nicholas Pope: the Sacred and the Profane*
Jonathan Vickery 2003 12pp 8 b&w illustrations
£2.00 ISBN 1 900081 24 5

44 *First Things: Sculpture and Maternity*
Anne M Wagner 2004 12pp 11 b&w illustrations
£2.00 ISBN 1 900081 44 X

45 *The Break-Up of New British Sculpture*
Antony Hudek 2005 16pp 6 illustrations (1 colour)
£2.00 ISBN 1 900081 54 7

46 *Medieval and Modern: Direct Carving In the Work of Gill and Barlach*
Irena Kossowska and Susanne Deicher 2005 16pp
13 b&w illustrations £2.00 ISBN 1 900081 59 8

47 *Passing By: Architectural Sculpture in Inter-War London*
Dennis Wardleworth 2005 16pp
10 b&w illustrations £2.00 ISBN 1 900081 49 0

48 *Shallow Space: Modernism's Civilising Norm*
Brandon Taylor 2005 12pp 10 b&w illustrations
£2.00 ISBN 1 900081 69 5

49 *Thomas Woolner: Seeing Sculpture Through Photography*
Joanne Lukitsh 2006 16pp 14 b&w illustrations
£2.00 ISBN 1 900081 94 6

50 *The Sculpture of Stephen Gilbert and Jocelyn Chewett in Post-War Paris*
Jon Wood, Hester R.Westley and Catherine Coughlan 2006 20pp 18 illustrations (14 colour)
£2.00 ISBN 1 905462 01 8

51 *Sensing Sculpture at the time of the French Revolution*
Valerie Mainz and Richard Williams 2006 12pp 9 b&w illustrations £2.00 ISBN 1 905462 07 7

52 *The 'Open Secret' of Alfred Gilbert's Male Nudes*
Jason Edwards 2006 12pp 12 illustrations (2 colour) £2.00 ISBN 1 905462 06 9

53 *Ian Breakwell's Unword, 1969-70: early performance art in Britain*
Victoria Worsley 2006 16pp 22 b&w illustrations
£2.00 ISBN 1 905462 05 0

54 *Russian Berlin in the 1920's*
Michael White and Paul Paret 2006 16pp 6 illustrations (2 colour) £2.00 ISBN 1 305462 08 5

55 *Drawing on Sculpture: Graphic Interventions on the Photographic Surface*
Jon Wood 2007 12pp 11 illustrations (6 colour)
£2.00 ISBN 978 1 905462 14 8

56 *Indoors and Out: The Sculpture and Design of Bernard Schottlander*
Catherine Moriarty, Victoria Worsley 2007 16pp 18 b&w illustrations £2.00 ISBN 978 1 905462 16 2

57 *A Kick in the Teeth: The Equestrian Monument to 'Field Marshal Earl Haig, Commander-in-Chief of the British Armies in France 1915-18' by Alfred Hardiman*
Nicholas Watkins 2008 12pp 13 b&w illustrations
£2.00 ISBN 978 1 905462 17 9

58 *By Leafy Ways: Early Works by Ivor Abrahams*
Sophie Raikes 2008 12pp 19 illustrations (2 colour)
£2.00 ISBN 978 1 905462 20 9

59 *Prospects and Interiors: Sculptors' Drawings of Inner Space*
Sophie Raikes 2008 12pp 17 illustrations (8 colour)
£2.00 ISBN 978 1 905462 22 3

60 *The Sculpture in the Home Exhibitions: Reconstructing the Home and Family in Post-War Britain*
Robert Burstow 2008 16pp 25 illustrations £2.00
ISBN 978 1 905462 24 7

61 *Box, Body, Burial: The Sculptural Imagination of Keith Arnatt*
Jon Wood, Mike Sperlinger, Andrew Wilson 2009 20pp 23 illustrations £2.00 ISBN 978 1 905462 26 1

62 *A Rough Equivalent: Sculpture and Pottery in the Post-War Period*
Jeffrey Jones 2010 20pp 23 illustrations £2.00
ISBN 978 1 905462 33 9

63 *Mario Merz: What Is to Be Done?*
Lisa Le Feuvre 2011 32pp 15 colour illustrations
£5.00 ISBN 978 1 905462 36 0